17
mf
O - ver the riv - er and through the wood, Oh,
21
how the wind does blow! It
f
25
stings the toes and bites the nose. As
29
o - ver the ground we go.
AF349121

Perky Turkey

Ladonna J. Weston

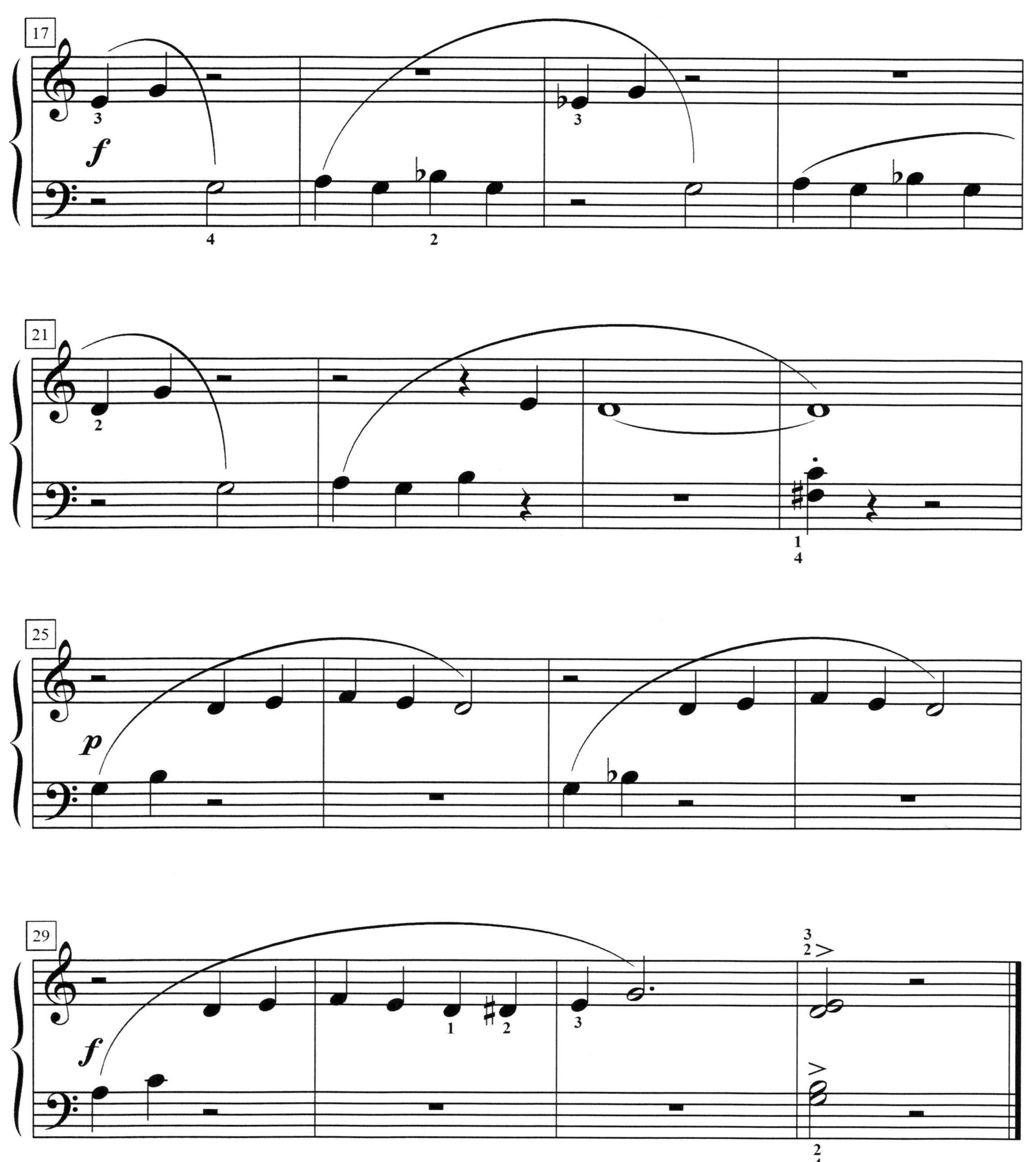

We Gather Together

On the First Thanksgiving Day

Jakob Hintz
Lyrics adapted by John W. Schaum

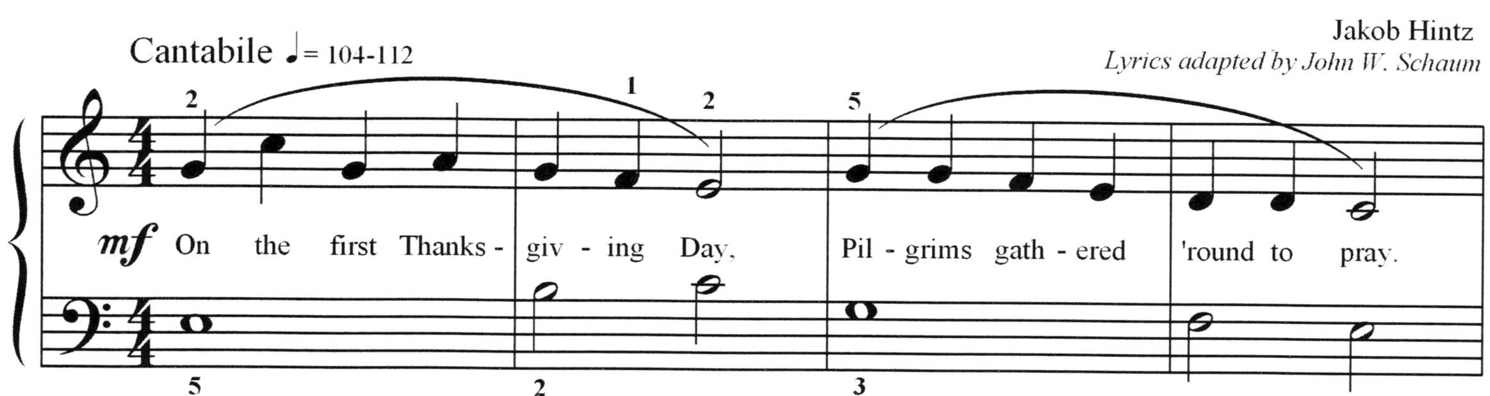

Harvest Song

(Swing the Shining Sickle)

Andantino ♩ = 104-112

Jessie Gaynor

* A *sickle* is a large knife with a curved blade, used for cutting stalks of grain at harvest time.
Sheaves are tied bunches of stalks of grain, after cutting.

9
mp Loud - ly blows the north wind, Through the shiv'-ring trees,
Bare are all the branch - es, Fall - en all the leaves.
mf Gath - ered is the har - vest For an - oth - er year,
f Now our day of glad - ness, Thanks-giv - ing Day is here.

Thanksgiving Parade